To: _____

From: _____

D0966783

THE WICKED WIT OF
JANE AUSTEN

THE WICKED WIT OF
JANE AUSTEN

Compiled, edited and introduced by

Dominique Enright

Michael O'Mara Books Limited

This revised edition
first published in Great Britain in 2011 by
Michael O'Mara Books Limited
9 Lion Yard
Tremadoc Road
London SW4 7NQ

A CIP catalogue record for this book
is available from the British Library

Papers used by Michael O'Mara Books Limited are natural,
recyclable products made from wood grown in sustainable forests.
The manufacturing processes conform to the environmental
regulations of the country of origin.

ISBN 978-1-84317-567-4

3 5 7 9 10 8 6 4 2

www.mombooks.com

Designed and typeset by Design 23

Cover image of Jane Austen from an engraving

Printed and bound in Great Britain by Clays Ltd, St Ives plc

Contents

Introduction 7

A Note on the Novels 13

Dramatis Personae 15

In a Manner Truly Heroick:
Early Exuberances 17

A Great Deal of It Must Be Invention:
History 25

Another Stupid Party:
Balls, Gowns and Other Fashions 31

In a Fine Burst of Literary Enthusiasm:
Books and Writing 47

The Rich Are Always Respectable 63

A Truth Universally Acknowledged:
The Marriage Market 69

The Nature of Their Attachments:
Men and Women							83

Jane Austen In Love – And Not					91

A Neighbourhood of Voluntary Spies:
Friends and Acquaintances					99

Vanity Working on a Weak Head:
Affectation and Arrogance					109

The Dissipations of London,
the Luxuries of Bath						119

A Fine Family							125

One Half Cannot Understand the Other:
Observations General and Particular			135

I Am a Very Good Housekeeper				153

Works by Jane Austen						159

Introduction

Jane Austen was born in 1775 to a country parson, George Austen, rector of Steventon in Hampshire, and his wife Cassandra. The lively, generally happy family with eight children, six of them boys, lived in a ramshackle rectory, which they shared with several pupils of a school run by the Austens. 'The Mansion of Learning', wrote Mrs Austen, 'where we study all day. Except when we play' seems to have been a cheerful place to grow up in, with much affection and laughter. The Austen sons were taught by their father along with the other boys; it was surely a matter for regret to Jane and her older sister Cassandra that they could not attend the school too – though they must have absorbed a great deal of learning by osmosis. The education of girls at that time was limited, though Jane and Cassandra were sent to boarding school for a few years to learn what was considered the essential basics for young ladies. From 1786 they stayed at home, where their informal education was probably a great deal better. 'I think I may boast myself, with all possible vanity, the most unlearned and uninformed female that ever dared to be an authoress,' Jane Austen later declared.

As is clear from her books she was neither. Brought up in an atmosphere of literary intelligence, surrounded by books of all kinds, a bright child could not but learn. Jane read widely and avidly – especially eighteenth-century writers such as Johnson, Goldsmith, Richardson, Fielding, Fanny Burney, Sterne – but she and the rest of her family also happily devoured the lighter novels of the day, novels 'of Terror' and 'of Sentiment' (the equivalents of today's paperback horror and romance) – the absurdity of the plots of the sillier ones (which she parodied in her early spoofs and ridiculed in *Northanger Abbey*) providing a fine source of entertainment.

'Of events her life was singularly barren: few changes and no great crisis ever broke the smooth current of its course,' wrote Jane Austen's nephew, James-Edward Austen-Leigh. And it has become accepted that Jane Austen led a very dull, sheltered life, a life ignorant of world events and of social deprivations, which she filled by writing books in which nothing much happens, that are a vehicle for sharp, witty comments on the narrow band of society she knew. Unremarkable as her life was, it was no more uneventful than that of most people: true, she never travelled abroad, but she had a huge extended family, and would often go to stay with some relation or other. She was fond of her many nieces and nephews, to whom she was a joyful and sympathetic companion: 'I have always maintained the importance of aunts,' she once remarked.

Jane Austen's life was not that removed from the wider world – it would have been difficult not to be aware of the French Revolution and the Napoleonic Wars rumbling in the near distance, for instance, and she kept in constant touch with her army-officer brother and with her two naval-officer brothers on their travels. But Austen simply chose not to write about these subjects: '3 or 4 families in a country village is the very thing to work on,' she wrote to her niece Anna, seeing in these few representative families, mainly country gentry, enough variety, enough of human vanities, frailties and foolishnesses, to reflect universal human traits.

From her letters it would seem as though her life was a mad social whirl – accounts of balls, visits and parties proliferate, described with a combination of exaggerated fancy and detached amusement. But life was not that cosy – poverty and illness presented a much greater threat – especially to women – than they do today. A middle-class woman was dependent upon her family or her husband. For a woman of any 'gentility' to work for her living was virtually inconceivable – hard times forced some to become, say, governesses, but there was little on offer.

Jane Austen was not without suitors. 'At length the day is come on which I am to flirt my last with Tom Lefroy, and when you receive this it will be over. My tears flow at the melancholy idea,' she wrote flippantly to Cassandra, following the departure of a family friend. Yet she seems to have expected him to propose, and might well have accepted – but did not press the matter when he had to go away, just mocking herself instead; another young man – met one summer – might have captured her heart, but he died before they could meet again. Was it the memories of these young men, or solidarity with

Cassandra, whose heart was broken when her fiancé died, that made her change her mind, when Harris Bigg-Wither, brother of friends of hers, proposed to her, and she accepted, only to tell him the next day that she had made a mistake and could not marry him? Or did she not want to lose the comparative freedom of her life, now that she was writing seriously, although very much in secret?

Along with meticulous observation and a keen eye for absurdity, it is a cool, dry irony that characterizes Jane Austen's mature writing. An unrestrained delight in the eccentricities of human nature is very evident in her youthful writing, where – often parodying the popular fiction of the day – she allowed herself to be as silly and ridiculous as she wanted, producing innumerable jokey poems and high-spirited stories and skits to entertain her family and friends, or for them to perform. In her later writing the boisterousness has largely been replaced by wit sometimes so sharp that it is almost unnoticed – but she did not entirely abandon the outrageously comic characters of her early work, merely refined them: Mr Collins in *Pride and Prejudice*, for example, is a caricature of fatuous and obsequious self-importance.

A keen watcher of other people's behaviour, she noted their mannerisms, and with her alert mind saw easily through weaknesses, pretension and affectation. Living at the edge of country gentry – her mother was quite 'well connected' – Jane Austen had many opportunities to observe the ways of the well-off and well-born. While she did not always admire their customs, she recognized and understood the power of social position and the security of money all too well – her own family was far from affluent. But it is too easy to see her novels as merely comic mockery of mankind: there is also a strong moral thread running through them. The arrogant characters are brought down a peg or two; the greedy lose out, the wicked get what they deserve (even if it is no worse than a silly wife gained and a fortune lost), fools and hypocrites are shown to be fools and hypocrites, marriages for money or position, rather than based on love and affection, are shown to be empty, assumptions are dismantled.

Jane Austen died in 1817 aged only forty-one, after an illness – identified variously as Addison's disease, Hodgkin's disease, and tuberculosis – against which she fought long and uncomplainingly. She wrote six novels, four of which were published in her lifetime. Her success as a writer lies in that, although her world was small, what she drew from it, and her insights into the people she encountered, allows her novels to function as microcosms for society at large. The keen comedy of her work continues to be as fresh today as when the novels were first published.

Just some of her sharpest, most profound and amusing observations taken from her early works, novels and letters are collected here, to inspire laughter, thought – and the odd wry grin of recognition. To explain the context of every quotation would defeat the purpose of this book – especially as many of Jane Austen's comments may be read and enjoyed out of context, even if altered slightly in meaning. On the whole, however, it is soon clear to the discerning reader as to whether some statement is ironic or not. As for the letters – Anne Elliot in *Persuasion* recognizes that 'no private correspondence could bear the eye of others' – and if some of the quotations from them seem quite outrageous, it should be remembered that Austen was writing to those close to her, usually Cassandra, who would understand what she meant – and whom she was trying to amuse.

DOMINIQUE ENRIGHT

A Note on the Novels

In the case of the published novels, the dates given are those of first publication: however, the dates do not necessarily reflect when they were written. The dates given for other of JA's writings indicate – as far as it is known – when they were written.

Elinor and Marianne was written in 1795–6, rewritten as *Sense and Sensibility* in 1797–8, revised in 1809, and published in 1811.

First Impressions was written in 1797, rewritten as *Pride and Prejudice* in 1809, and published in 1813.

Mansfield Park was begun in 1811 and published in 1814.

Emma was begun in 1814 and published in 1816.

Susan was begun around 1798 and was sold to a publisher, Richard Crosby, in 1803, who, beyond advertising it, did nothing. JA was only able to buy it back in 1816, when she renamed the heroine Catherine, by which name the book became known, and wrote a prefatory note to it. It was not published until 1818, and under the title *Northanger Abbey*.

Persuasion, begun in 1815, was published in 1818.

The Watsons was begun in 1804, but abandoned in 1805 with George Austen's death. (The father of the Watson sisters in the novel was to die – possibly a reason for JA's abandonment of the novel when her own father died.)

Sanditon was begun in 1817; JA died before she could finish it.

For ease of reading Jane Austen's spelling and her use of capitals have, in general, been standardized, although in a few instances – for example her preference for 'ei', as in 'freindship' – original spellings have been retained for flavour. Her ampersands have been replaced by 'and'.

Dramatis Personae

Recipients of the letters quoted here:

CASSANDRA: Cassandra Austen (1773–1845), JA's sister

FRANK: Francis Austen (1774–1865), JA's brother, nearest to her in age

FANNY KNIGHT (1793–1882), JA's niece, daughter of brother Edward Knight; in 1829 she married Sir Edward Knatchbull

ANNA AUSTEN (1793–1872), JA's niece, daughter of James; she married Ben Lefroy in 1814

EDWARD AUSTEN-LEIGH: JA's nephew James-Edward Austen-Leigh (1798–1874), son of James, half-brother of Anna

CAROLINE AUSTEN (1805–80), JA's niece, daughter of James and sister of Edward

MARTHA LLOYD (1765–1843), lifelong friend of the family, who in 1828 became Frank Austen's second wife

JAMES STANIER CLARKE, the Prince Regent's librarian at Carlton House

In a Manner Truly Heroick: Early Exuberances

They said he was sensible, well-informed, and agreeable; we did not pretend to judge of such trifles, but as we were convinced he had no soul, that he had never read *The Sorrows of Werther*, and that his Hair bore not the least resemblance to auburn, we were certain that Janetta could feel no affection for him, or at least that she ought to feel none. The very circumstance of his being her father's choice too, was so much in his disfavour, that . . . *that* of itself ought to have been a sufficient reason in the eyes of Janetta for rejecting him.

LOVE AND FREINDSHIP, 1790

[Cassandra's] father was of noble birth, being the near relation of the Duchess of ——'s Butler.

THE BEAUTIFULL CASSANDRA, ?1789

[Chapter 4] She then proceeded to a Pastry-cook's, where she devoured six ices, refused to pay for them, knocked down the pastry cook and walked away . . .

THE BEAUTIFULL CASSANDRA, ?1789

[Chapter 6] Being returned to the same spot of the same street she had set out from, the coachman demanded his pay . . .
THE BEAUTIFULL CASSANDRA, ?1789

[Chapter 7] She searched her pockets over again and again; but every search was unsuccessful. No money could she find. The man grew peremptory. She placed her bonnet on his head and ran away.
THE BEAUTIFULL CASSANDRA, ?1789

Gently brawling down the turnpike road,
Sweetly noisy falls the Silent Stream.
'ODE TO PITY', 1787/90

But lovely as I was, the graces of my person were the least of my perfections. Of every accomplishment accustomary to my sex, I was mistress.
LOVE AND FREINDSHIP, 1790

In Lady Williams every virtue met. She was a widow with a handsome jointure and the remains of a very handsome face. Though benevolent and candid, she was generous and sincere; though pious and good, she was religious and amiable, and though elegant and agreeable, she was polished and entertaining.

JACK AND ALICE, 1787/90

Never did I see such an affecting scene as was the meeting of Edward and Augustus.
'My life! my soul!' (exclaimed the former) 'My adorable angel!' (replied the latter), as they flew into each other's arms. It was too pathetic for the feelings of Sophia and myself –
We fainted alternately on a sofa.

LOVE AND FREINDSHIP, 1790

One fatal swoon has cost me my Life . . . Beware of swoons, Dear Laura . . . A frenzy fit is not one quarter so pernicious; it is an exercise to the body and if not too violent, is, I dare say, conducive to health in its consequences – run mad as often as you chuse; but do not faint . . .

LOVE AND FREINDSHIP, 1790

[*A coach arrives*] A gentleman considerably advanced in years, descended from it. At his first appearance my sensibility was wonderfully affected, and e'er I had gazed at him a second time, an instinctive sympathy whispered to my heart that he was my grandfather.

LOVE AND FREINDSHIP, 1790

In half a year he returned and set off in the stage coach for Hogsworth Green, the seat of Emma. His fellow travellers were, A man without a hat, Another with two, An old maid, and a young wife. This last appeared about 17, with fine dark eyes and an elegant shape; in short, Mr Harley soon found out that she was his Emma and recollected he had married her a few weeks before he left England.

'THE ADVENTURES OF MR HARLEY', ?1789/90

Miss Fitzgerald: Bless me! there ought to be 8 chairs and there are but 6. However, if your Ladyship will but take Sir Arthur in your lap, and Sophy my brother in hers, I believe we shall do pretty well.

THE VISIT, A COMEDY IN 2 ACTS, 1787/90

Lord Fitzgerald: I am afraid you found your bed too short.
It was bought in my grandmother's time, who was herself
a very short woman and made a point of suiting all her beds
to her own length, as she never wished to have any company
in the house . . .
THE VISIT, A COMEDY IN 2 ACTS, 1787/90

Miss Fitzgerald: I am really shocked at crowding you in such a
manner, but my grandmother (who bought all the furniture
of this room) as she had never a very large party, did not
think it necessary to buy more chairs than were sufficient for
her own family and two of her particular friends . . .
THE VISIT, A COMEDY IN 2 ACTS, 1787/90

Lord Fitzgerald: I wish we had any dessert to offer you.
But my grandmother in her lifetime, destroyed the hothouse
in order to build a receptacle for the turkeys with its
materials; and we have never been able to raise another
tolerable one.
THE VISIT, A COMEDY IN 2 ACTS, 1787/90

'Miss Dickins was an excellent governess. She instructed me in the paths of virtue; under her tuition I daily became more amiable, and might perhaps by this time have nearly obtained perfection, had not my worthy preceptoress been torn from my arms, e'er I had attained my seventeenth year. I never shall forget her last words. "My dear Kitty" she said "Good night t'ye." I never saw her afterwards,' continued Lady Williams wiping her eyes. 'She eloped with the butler the same night.'
JACK AND ALICE, 1787/90

... My Mother rode upon our little pony, and Fanny and I walked by her side or rather ran, for my Mother is so fond of riding fast that she galloped all the way. You may be sure that we were in a fine perspiration when we came to our place of resting. Fanny has taken a great many drawings of the country, which are very beautiful, tho' perhaps not such exact resemblances as might be wished, from their being taken as she ran along ...
'A TOUR THROUGH WALES
– IN A LETTER FROM A YOUNG LADY'

A Great Deal of It
Must Be Invention:
History

'It tells me nothing that does not either vex or weary me. The quarrels of popes and kings, with wars or pestilences, in every page; the men all so good for nothing, and hardly any women at all – it is very tiresome: and yet I often think it odd that it should be so dull, for a great deal of it must be invention. The speeches that are put into the heroes' mouths, their thoughts and designs – the chief of all this must be invention . . .'

CATHERINE MORLAND,
NORTHANGER ABBEY, 1818

'Queen Elizabeth,' said Mrs Stanley, who never hazarded a remark on history that was not well founded, 'lived to a good old age, and was a very clever woman.'

CATHARINE, 1792

A selection, dated 1791, from a distinctly individual view, dedicated to and illustrated by Cassandra Austen:

THE HISTORY OF ENGLAND FROM THE REIGN OF HENRY THE 4TH TO THE DEATH OF CHARLES THE 1ST

By a partial, prejudiced, and ignorant Historian
NB There will be very few dates in this history

HENRY THE 4TH

Henry the 4th ascended the throne of England much to his own satisfaction in the year 1399, after having prevailed on his cousin and predecessor Richard the 2d to resign it to him, and to retire for the rest of his Life to Pomfret Castle, where he happened to be murdered.

HENRY THE 6TH

I cannot say much for this Monarch's sense – nor would I if I could, for he was a Lancastrian. I suppose you know all about the Wars between him and the Duke of York, who was of the right side; if you do not, you had better read some other History, for I shall not be very diffuse in this, meaning by it only to vent my spleen *against*, and show my hatred *to* all those people whose parties or principles do not suit with mine, and not to give information . . . It was in this reign that Joan of Arc lived and made such a row among the English. They should not have burnt her – but they did . . .

EDWARD THE 4TH

This Monarch was famous only for his beauty and his courage, of which the picture we have here given of him, and his undaunted behaviour in marrying one woman while he was engaged to another, are sufficient proofs ... One of Edward's mistresses was Jane Shore, who has had a play written about her, but it is a tragedy and therefore not worth reading ...

HENRY THE 8TH

The crimes and cruelties of this prince were too numerous to be mentioned (as this history I trust has fully shown); and nothing can be said in his vindication, but that his abolishing religious houses and leaving them to the ruinous depredations of time has been of infinite use to the landscape of England in general, which probably was a principal motive for his doing it, since otherwise why should a man who was of no religion himself be at so much trouble to abolish one which had for ages been established in the Kingdom?

ELIZABETH

It was the peculiar misfortune of this woman to have had bad ministers – since wicked as she herself was, she could not have committed such extensive mischeif, had not these vile and abandoned men connived at, and encouraged her in her crimes . . . It was about this time that Sir Francis Drake the first English navigator who sailed round the world, lived, to be the ornament of his country and his profession. Yet great as he was, and justly celebrated as a sailor, I cannot help foreseeing that he will be equalled in this or the next century by one who tho' now but young, already promises to answer all the ardent and sanguine expectations of his relations and freinds, amongst whom I may class the amiable lady to whom this work is dedicated, and my no less amiable self.

EDWARD THE 6TH

As this prince was only nine years old at the time of his Father's death, he was considered by many people as too young to govern, and the late King happening to be of the same opinion, his mother's brother, the Duke of Somerset, was chosen Protector of the realm during his minority . . . He was beheaded, of which he might with reason have been proud, had he known that such was [to be] the death of Mary Queen of Scotland; but as it was impossible that he should be conscious of what had never happened, it does not appear that he felt particularly delighted with the manner of it . . .

CHARLES THE 1ST

. . . The events of this Monarch's reign are too numerous for my pen, and indeed the recital of any events (except what I make myself) is uninteresting to me . . .

Another Stupid Party: Balls, Gowns and Other Fashions

'I remember I met Miss Dudley last spring with Lady Amyatt at Ranelagh, and she had such a frightful cap on, that I have never been able to bear any of them since.'
CATHARINE, 1792

Mrs Badcock and two young women were of the same party, except when Mrs Badcock thought herself obliged to leave them to run round the room after her drunken husband. His avoidance, and her pursuit, with the probable intoxication of both, was an amusing scene.
LETTER TO CASSANDRA, 12–13 MAY 1801

Our ball was chiefly made up of Jervoises and Terrys, the former of whom were apt to be vulgar, the latter to be noisy. I had an odd set of partners: Mr Jenkins, Mr Street, Col. Jervoise, James Digweed, J. Lyford, and Mr Biggs, a friend of the latter. I had a very pleasant evening, however, though you will probably find out that there was no particular reason for it.
LETTER TO CASSANDRA, 21–3 JANUARY 1799

On every formal visit a child ought to be of the party, by way of provision for discourse. In the present case it took up ten minutes to determine whether the boy were most like his father or mother, and in what particular he resembled either, for of course every body differed, and every body was astonished at the opinion of the others.

SENSE AND SENSIBILITY, 1811

There were very few beauties, and such as there were not very handsome . . . Mrs Blount was the only one much admired. She appeared exactly as she did in September, with the same broad face, diamond bandeau, white shoes, pink husband, and fat neck.

LETTER TO CASSANDRA, 20–1 NOVEMBER 1800

'The sooner every party breaks up, the better.'
MR WOODHOUSE, *EMMA*, 1816

'One cannot have too large a party. A large party secures its own amusement.'
EMMA, *EMMA*, 1816

There were only twelve dances, of which I danced nine, and was merely prevented from dancing the rest by want of a partner ...
LETTER TO CASSANDRA, 20–1 NOVEMBER 1800

Another stupid party last night; perhaps if larger they might be less intolerable, but here there were only just enough to make one card-table, with six people to look on and talk nonsense to each other. Lady Fust, Mrs Busby, and a Mrs Owen sat down with my uncle to whist, within five minutes after the three old *Toughs* came in, and there they sat, with only the exchange of Adm. Stanhope for my uncle, till their chairs were announced.
LETTER TO CASSANDRA, 12–13 MAY 1801

The elegant stupidity of private parties.
PERSUASION, 1818

Mrs Lefroy has just sent me word that Lady Dorchester
means to invite me to her ball on January 8, which, though
an humble blessing compared with what the last page records,
I do not consider as any calamity.
LETTER TO CASSANDRA, 28 DECEMBER 1798

On Wednesday morning it was settled that Mrs Harwood,
Mary, and I should go together, and shortly afterwards a very
civil note of invitation for me came from Mrs Bramston,
who wrote I believe as soon as she knew of the ball. I might
likewise have gone with Mrs Lefroy, and therefore, with three
methods of going, I must have been more at the ball than
anyone else.
LETTER TO CASSANDRA, 1 NOVEMBER 1800

Another Stupid Party

Our ball on Thursday was a very poor one, only eight couple and but twenty-three people in the room; but it was not the ball's fault.
LETTER TO CASSANDRA, 21–3 JANUARY 1799

I had the comfort of finding out the other evening who all the fat girls with short noses were that disturbed me at the 1st H. ball. They all prove to be Miss Atkinsons of Enham.
LETTER TO CASSANDRA, 30 NOVEMBER – 1 DECEMBER 1800

Your silence on the subject of our ball makes me suppose your curiosity too great for words. We were very well entertained, and could have stayed longer but for the arrival of my list [cloth] shoes to convey me home, and I did not like to keep them waiting in the cold.
LETTER TO CASSANDRA, 24 JANUARY 1809

Yes, I mean to go to as many balls as possible, that I may have a good bargain.
LETTER TO CASSANDRA, 9 DECEMBER 1808

I was very glad to be spared the trouble of dressing and going, and being weary before it was half over.
LETTER TO CASSANDRA, 14–15 OCTOBER 1813

It may be possible to do without dancing entirely. Instances have been known of young people passing many, many months successively, without being at any ball of any description, and no material injury accrue either to body or mind; – but when a beginning is made – when the felicities of rapid motion have once been, though slightly, felt – it must be a very heavy set that does not ask for more.
EMMA, 1816

I suppose the Ashford ball will furnish something.
LETTER TO CASSANDRA, 11–12 OCTOBER 1813

It was a delightful visit; – perfect, in being much too short.
EMMA, 1816

[Fashionable schools] where young ladies for enormous pay
might be screwed out of health and into vanity.
EMMA, 1816

I continue quite well; in proof of which I have
bathed again this morning. It was absolutely
necessary that I should have the little fever and
indisposition which I had: it has been all the
fashion this week in Lyme.
LETTER TO CASSANDRA, 14 SEPTEMBER 1804

It is the fashion to think [Mrs and Miss Holder] both very detestable, but they are so civil, and their gowns look so white and so nice (which, by the bye, my aunt thinks an absurd pretension in this place), that I cannot utterly abhor them.

LETTER TO CASSANDRA, 21–2 MAY 1801

She was nothing more than a mere good-tempered, civil and obliging young woman; as such we could scarcely dislike her – she was only an Object of Contempt.

LOVE AND FREINDSHIP, 1790

Woman is fine for her own satisfaction alone. No man will admire her the more, no woman will like her the better for it. Neatness and fashion are enough for the former, and a something of shabbiness or impropriety will be most endearing to the latter.

NORTHANGER ABBEY, 1818

I bought some Japan ink likewise, and next week shall begin
my operations on my hat, on which you know my principal
hopes of happiness depend.
LETTER TO CASSANDRA, 27–8 OCTOBER 1798

I find great comfort in my stuff gown, but I hope you do not
wear yours too often. I have made myself two or three caps
to wear of evenings since I came home, and they save me a
world of torment as to hair-dressing, which at present gives
me no trouble beyond washing and brushing,
LETTER TO CASSANDRA, 1–2 DECEMBER 1798

I cannot determine what to do about my new gown; I wish
such things were to be bought ready-made.
LETTER TO CASSANDRA, 24–6 DECEMBER 1798

My black cap was openly admired by Mrs Lefroy, and secretly I imagine by everybody else in the room.

LETTER TO CASSANDRA, 24–6 DECEMBER 1798

. . . the purchase of a new muslin gown . . . *I* am determined to buy a handsome one whenever I can, and I am so tired and ashamed of half my present stock, that I even blush at the sight of the wardrobe which contains them. But I will not be much longer libelled by the possession of my coarse spot; I shall turn it into a petticoat very soon. I wish you a merry Christmas, but no compliments of the season.

LETTER TO CASSANDRA, 24–6 DECEMBER 1798

I am not to wear my white satin cap to-night, after all; I am to wear a Mamalouc cap instead, which Charles Fowle sent to Mary, and which she lends me. It is all the fashion now; worn at the opera, and by Lady Mildmays at Hackwood balls. I hate describing such things, and I dare say you will be able to guess what it is like. I have got over the dreadful epocha of mantuamaking much better than I expected.

LETTER TO CASSANDRA, 8–9 JANUARY 1799

Though you have given me unlimited powers concerning your sprig, I cannot determine what to do about it ... I cannot help thinking that it is more natural to have flowers grow out of the head than fruit. What do you think on that subject?
LETTER TO CASSANDRA, 11 JUNE 1799

My hair was at least tidy, which was all my ambition.
LETTER TO CASSANDRA, 20–1 NOVEMBER 1800

Dress is at all times a frivolous distinction, and excessive solicitude about it often destroys its own aim.
NORTHANGER ABBEY, 1818

Mrs Powlett was at once expensively nakedly dressed; we have had the satisfaction of estimating her lace and her muslin; and she said too little to afford us much other amusement.
LETTER TO CASSANDRA, 8 JANUARY 1801

'A simple style of dress is so infinitely preferable to finery. But I am quite in the minority, I believe; few people seem to value simplicity of dress, – show and finery are every thing.'
MRS ELTON, *EMMA*, 1816

I learnt from Mrs Tickars's young lady, to my high amusement, that the stays now are not made to force the bosom up at all; *that* was a very unbecoming, unnatural fashion. I was really glad to hear that they are not to be so much off the shoulders as they were.
LETTER TO CASSANDRA, 15 SEPTEMBER 1813

You really must get some flounces. Are not some of your large stock of white morning gowns just in a happy state for a flounce – too short?
LETTER TO CASSANDRA, 14–15 OCTOBER 1813

I have determined to trim my lilac sarsenet with black satin ribbon just as my China crape is, 6*d*. width at the bottom, 3*d*. or 4*d*., at top. Ribbon trimmings are all the fashion at Bath, and I dare say the fashions of the two places are alike enough in that point to content me. With this addition it will be a very useful gown, happy to go anywhere.

LETTER TO CASSANDRA, 5–8 MARCH, 1814

It would be mortifying to the feelings of many ladies, could they be made to understand how little the heart of man is affected by what is costly or new in their attire; how little it is biased by the texture of their muslin, and how unsusceptible of peculiar tenderness towards the spotted, the sprigged, the mull, or the jackonet.

NORTHANGER ABBEY, 1818

Man only can be aware of the insensibility of man towards a new gown.

NORTHANGER ABBEY, 1818

I am amused by the present style of female dress; – the coloured petticoats with braces over the white spencers and enormous bonnets upon the full stretch, are quite entertaining. It seems to me a more marked *change* than one has lately seen. – Long sleeves appear universal, even as *dress*, the waists short, and, as far as I have been able to judge, the bosom covered.

LETTER TO MARTHA LLOYD,
FROM LONDON, 2 SEPTEMBER 1814

In a Fine Burst of Literary Enthusiasm: Books and Writing

As an inducement to subscribe, Mrs Martin [running the circulating-library] tells me that her collection is not to consist only of novels, but of every kind of literature, etc etc. She might have spared this pretension to *our* family, who are great novel-readers and not ashamed of being so; but it was necessary, I suppose, to the self-consequence of half her subscribers.

<small>LETTER TO CASSANDRA, 18–19 DECEMBER 1798</small>

'I think you must like Udolpho, if you were to read it; it is so very interesting.'
'Not I, faith! No, if I read any, it shall be Mrs Radcliffe's; her novels are amusing enough;
they are worth reading; some fun and nature in them.'
'Udolpho was written by Mrs Radcliffe,' said Catherine, with some hesitation, from the fear of mortifying him.

<small>CATHERINE MORLAND AND JOHN THORPE,
NORTHANGER ABBEY, 1818</small>

We had a Miss North and a Mr Gould of our party; the latter walked home with me after tea. He is a very young man, just entered of Oxford, wears spectacles, and has heard that *Evelina* was written by Dr Johnson.
LETTER TO CASSANDRA, 2 JUNE 1799

Because they were fond of reading, she fancied them satirical: perhaps without exactly knowing what it was to be satirical; but that did not signify.
SENSE AND SENSIBILITY, 1811

Provided that nothing like useful knowledge could be gained from them, provided they were all story and no reflection, she had never any objection to books at all.
NORTHANGER ABBEY, 1818, OF CATHERINE MORLAND

'But you never read novels, I dare say?'
'Why not?'
'Because they are not clever enough for you –
gentlemen read better books.'
'The person, be it gentleman or lady, who has not
pleasure in a good novel, must be intolerably stupid.'
CATHERINE MORLAND AND HENRY TILNEY,
NORTHANGER ABBEY, 1818

'I am no indiscriminate novel-reader. The mere trash of the
common circulating library, I hold in the highest contempt.
You will never hear me advocating those puerile emanations
which detail nothing but discordant principles incapable of
amalgamation, or those vapid tissues of ordinary occurrences
from which no useful deductions can be drawn. – In vain
may we put them into a literary alembic; – we distil nothing
which can add to science.
You understand me I am sure?'
SIR EDWARD, *SANDITON*, 1817

The truth was that Sir Edward, whom circumstances had confined very much to one spot, had read more sentimental novels than agreed with him.

SANDITON, 1817

We have tried to get *Self-control*, but in vain. I *should* like to know what her estimate is, but am always half afraid of finding a clever novel *too clever*, and of finding my own story and my own people all forestalled.

LETTER TO CASSANDRA, 30 APRIL 1811

[I will write] a close imitation of Self-Control as soon as I can; – I will improve upon it; – my heroine shall not merely be wafted down an American river in a boat by herself, she shall cross the Atlantic in the same way and never stop till she reaches Gravesend.

LETTER TO ANNA LEFROY (AUSTEN), LATE 1814/EARLY 1815

If people like to read their books, it is all very well, but to be at so much trouble in filling great volumes, which, as I used to think, nobody would willingly ever look into, to be labouring only for the torment of little boys and girls, always struck me as a hard fate.
CATHERINE MORLAND, *NORTHANGER ABBEY*, 1818

I am quite determined however not to be pleased with Mrs West's *Alicia de Lacy* [*an Historical Romance*], should I ever meet with it, which I hope I may not. – I think I *can* be stout against anything written by Mrs West. – I have made up my mind to like no novels really, but Miss Edgeworth's, yours and my own.
LETTER TO ANNA AUSTEN, 9–18 SEPTEMBER 1814

How good Mrs West [a prolific authoress] could have written such books and collected so many hard works, with all her family cares, is still more a matter of astonishment! Composition seems to me impossible with a head full of joints of mutton and doses of rhubarb.
LETTER TO CASSANDRA, 8–9 SEPTEMBER 1816

Walter Scott has no business to write novels, especially good ones. It is not fair. He has fame and profit enough as a poet, and should not be taking the bread out of the mouths of other people.

LETTER TO ANNA AUSTEN, 28 SEPTEMBER 1814

'Oh! It is only a novel!' replies the young lady, while she lays down her book with affected indifference, or momentary shame. 'It is only *Cecilia*, or *Camilla*, or *Belinda*'; or, in short, only some work in which the greatest powers of the mind are displayed, in which the most thorough knowledge of human nature, the happiest delineation of its varieties, the liveliest effusions of wit and humour, are conveyed to the world in the best-chosen language.

NORTHANGER ABBEY, 1818

I do not wonder at your wanting to read *First Impressions* again, so seldom as you have gone through it, and that so long ago.

LETTER TO CASSANDRA, 9 JANUARY 1799

Fanny and the two little girls . . . revelled last night in *Don Juan*, whom we left in Hell at half-past eleven . . . The girls . . . still prefer *Don Juan*; and I must say that I have seen nobody on the stage who has been a more interesting character than that compound of cruelty and lust.

LETTER TO CASSANDRA FROM LONDON, 15–16 SEPTEMBER 1813

I would not let Martha read *First Impressions* again upon any account, and am very glad that I did not leave it in your power. She is very cunning, but I saw through her design; she means to publish it from memory, and one more perusal must enable her to do it.

LETTER TO CASSANDRA, 11 JUNE 1799

I am very much flattered by your commendation of my last letter, for I write only for fame, and without any view to pecuniary emolument.

LETTER TO CASSANDRA, 14–15 JANUARY 1798

'A person who can write a long letter with ease,
cannot write ill.'
Miss Bingley, *Pride and Prejudice*, 1813

I could no more write a [historical] romance than an epic
poem. I could not sit seriously down to write a serious
romance under any other motive than to save my life, and
if it were indispensable for me to keep it up and never relax
into laughing at myself or other people, I am sure I should be
hung before I had finished the first chapter.
Letter to James Stanier Clarke, 1 April 1816

Poor Dr Isham is obliged to admire *P. and P.*, and to send
me word that he is sure he shall not like Madame D'Arblay's
[Fanny Burney's] new novel half so well. Mrs Cooke invented
it all, of course.
23–4 September 1813

[...] I want to tell you that I have got my own darling child [*Pride and Prejudice*] from London.
LETTER TO CASSANDRA, 29 JANUARY 1813

Lady Robert is delighted with *P. and P.*, and really *was* so, as I understand, before she knew who wrote it – for, of course, she knows now. He [Henry] told her with as much satisfaction as·if it were my wish.
LETTER TO CASSANDRA, 15–16 SEPTEMBER 1813

No, indeed, I am never too busy to think of *S. and S.* I can no more forget it than a mother can forget her sucking child.
LETTER TO CASSANDRA, 25 APRIL 1811

I dined upon goose yesterday, which, I hope, will secure a good sale of my second edition [of *Sense and Sensibility*].
LETTER TO CASSANDRA, 11–12 OCTOBER 1813

Since I wrote last, my 2nd edit. [of *Sense and Sensibility*] has stared me in the face … I cannot help hoping that *many* will feel themselves obliged to buy it. I shall not mind imagining it a disagreeable duty to them, so as they do it.

LETTER TO CASSANDRA, 6–7 NOVEMBER 1813

Henry has this moment said that he likes my *M[ansfield] P[ark]* better and better; – he is in the third volume. I believe *now* he has changed his mind as to foreseeing the end; he said yesterday, at least, that he defied anybody to say whether H[enry] C[rawford] would be reformed, or would forget Fanny in a fortnight.

LETTER TO CASSANDRA, 5–8 MARCH 1814

Perhaps before the end of April, *Mansfield Park* by the author of S and S – P and P may be in the world. – Keep the *name* to yourself, I should not like to have it known beforehand.

LETTER TO FRANK, 21 MARCH 1814

In addition to their standing claims on me they admire *Mansfield Park* exceedingly. Mr Cooke says 'it is the most sensible novel he ever read' and the manner in which I treat the clergy delights them very much.

LETTER TO CASSANDRA, 14 JUNE 1814

You will be glad to hear that the first edition of *M[ansfield] P[ark]* is all sold. Your uncle Henry is rather wanting me to come to town to settle about a second edition, but as I could not very conveniently leave home now, I have written him my will and pleasure, and, unless he still urges it, shall not go. I am very greedy and want to make the most of it, but as you are much above caring about money I shall not plague you with any particulars.

LETTER TO FANNY KNIGHT, 18–20 NOVEMBER 1814

I am strongly haunted with the idea that to those readers who have preferred *Pride and Prejudice*, [*Emma*] will appear inferior in wit, and to those who have preferred *Mansfield Park* inferior in good sense.

LETTER TO JAMES STANIER CLARKE, 11 DECEMBER 1815

Make everybody at Hendon admire *Mansfield Park*.
LETTER TO ANNA LEFROY (AUSTEN), 22 NOVEMBER 1814

I have just received nearly twenty pounds myself on the second edition of *Sense and Sensibility* which gives me fine flow of literary ardour.
LETTER TO CAROLINE AUSTEN, 14 MARCH 1817

Do not be surprised at finding Uncle Henry acquainted with my having another ready for publication. I could not say No when he asked me, but he knows nothing more of it. You will not like it, so you need not be impatient. You may *perhaps* like the heroine, as she is almost too good for me.
LETTER TO FANNY KNIGHT, 23–5 MARCH 1817
(THE NOVEL WAS *PERSUASION*.)

Let other pens dwell on guilt and misery. I quit such odious subjects as soon as I can, impatient to restore everybody, not greatly in fault themselves, to tolerable comfort, and to have done with all the rest.

MANSFIELD PARK, 1814

The Rich Are Always Respectable

'Business, you know, may bring money, but friendship hardly ever does.'
MR JOHN KNIGHTLEY, *EMMA*, 1816

This morning brought me a letter from Mrs Knight, containing the usual fee, and all the usual kindnesses. She asks me to spend a day or two with her this week . . . I sent my answer . . . which I wrote without much effort, for I was rich – and the rich are always respectable, whatever be their style of writing.
LETTER TO CASSANDRA, 20–2 JUNE 1808
(Mrs Knight, adoptive mother of JA's brother Edward, seems to have taken it upon herself to pay JA a regular allowance)

I find, on looking into my affairs, that instead of being very rich I am likely to be very poor . . . as we are to meet in Canterbury I need not have mentioned this. It is as well, however, to prepare you for the sight of a sister sunk in poverty, that it may not overcome your spirits.
LETTER TO CASSANDRA, 24 AUGUST 1805

People get so horridly poor and economical in this part of the world that I have no patience with them. Kent is the only place for happiness; everybody is rich there.

LETTER TO CASSANDRA, 18–19 DECEMBER 1798

'I am tolerably glad to hear that Edward's income is so good a one – as glad as I can be at anybody's being rich except you and me – and I am thoroughly rejoiced to hear of his present to you.'

LETTER TO CASSANDRA, 8–9 JANUARY 1799

'An annuity is a very serious business; it comes over and over every year, and there is no getting rid of it.'

MRS JOHN DASHWOOD, *SENSE AND SENSIBILITY*, 1811

A large income is the best recipe for happiness I ever heard of. It certainly may secure all the myrtle and turkey part of it.

MARY CRAWFORD, *MANSFIELD PARK*, 1814

'Money can only give happiness where there is nothing
else to give it.'
MARIANNE DASHWOOD, *SENSE AND SENSIBILITY*, 1811

P. and P. is sold. – Egerton gives £110 for it. – I would rather
have had £150, but we could not both be pleased, and I am
not at all surprised that he should not choose to hazard
so much.
LETTER TO MARTHA LLOYD, 29–30 NOVEMBER 1812

I was previously aware of what I should be laying
myself open to – but the truth is that the Secret
has spread so far as to be scarcely the shadow of
a secret now – and that I believe that whenever
the third appears, I shall not even attempt to tell
lies about it. – I shall rather try to make all the
money than all mystery I can of it.
LETTER TO FRANK, 25 SEPTEMBER 1813

'But if you observe, people always live for ever when there is an annuity to be paid them.'
MRS JOHN DASHWOOD, *SENSE AND SENSIBILITY*, 1811

'After all that romancers may say, there is no doing without money.'
ISABELLA THORPE, *NORTHANGER ABBEY*, 1818

'A single woman, with a very narrow income, must be a ridiculous, disagreeable, old maid! the proper sport of boys and girls; but a single woman, of good fortune, is always respectable, and may be as sensible and pleasant as anybody else.'
EMMA, *EMMA*, 1816

A Truth Universally Acknowledged: The Marriage Market

It is a truth universally acknowledged, that a single man in possession of a good fortune must be in want of a wife.
PRIDE AND PREJUDICE, 1813

However little known the feelings or views of such a man may be on his first entering a neighbourhood, this truth is so well fixed in the minds of the surrounding families, that he is considered as the rightful property of some one or other of their daughters.
PRIDE AND PREJUDICE, 1813

'Almost as soon as I entered the house, I singled you out as the companion of my future life. But before I am run away with by my feelings on this subject, perhaps it would be advisable for me to state my reasons for marrying – and moreover for coming into Hertfordshire with the design of selecting a wife, as I certainly did.'
MR COLLINS, *PRIDE AND PREJUDICE*, 1813

Mr Collins had only to change from Jane to Elizabeth, and it was soon done – done while Mrs Bennet was stirring the fire.
PRIDE AND PREJUDICE, 1813

It would be an excellent match, for *he* was rich, and *she* was handsome.
SENSE AND SENSIBILITY, 1811

Without thinking highly either of men or of matrimony, marriage had always been [Charlotte Lucas's] object; it was the only honourable provision for well-educated young women of small fortune, and however uncertain of giving happiness, must be their pleasantest preservative from want.
PRIDE AND PREJUDICE, 1813

'But you know we must marry . . . but my father cannot provide for us, and it is very bad to grow old and be poor and laughed at.'
ELIZABETH, *THE WATSONS*, 1804

'It is a manoeuvring business. I know so many
who have married in the full expectation and
confidence of some one particular advantage
in the connexion, or accomplishment, or good
quality in the person, who have found themselves
entirely deceived, and been obliged to put up with
exactly the reverse. What is this but a take-in?'
MARY CRAWFORD, *MANSFIELD PARK*, 1814

But there certainly are not so many men of large fortune in
the world as there are pretty women to deserve them.
MANSFIELD PARK, 1814

'Pray, my dear aunt, what is the difference in matrimonial
affairs, between the mercenary and the prudent motive?
Where does discretion end, and avarice begin?'
ELIZABETH BENNET, *PRIDE AND PREJUDICE*, 1813

'She is not the first girl who has gone to the East Indies for a husband, and I declare I should think it very good fun if I were as poor.'
CAMILLA, *CATHARINE*, 1792

Single women have a dreadful propensity for being poor – which is one very strong argument in favour of matrimony.
LETTER TO FANNY KNIGHT, 13 MARCH 1817

'Happiness in marriage is entirely a matter of chance.'
CHARLOTTE LUCAS, *PRIDE AND PREJUDICE*, 1813

In all the important preparations of the mind [Maria Bertram] was complete: being prepared for matrimony by an hatred of home, restraint, and tranquillity; by the misery of disappointed affection, and contempt of the man she was to marry.
MANSFIELD PARK, 1814

'In nine cases out of ten, a woman had better show *more* affection than she feels.'
CHARLOTTE LUCAS, *PRIDE AND PREJUDICE*, 1813

'In marriage especially . . . there is not one in a hundred of either sex who is not taken in when they marry. Look where I will, I see that it *is* so; and I feel that it *must* be so, when I consider that it is, of all transactions, the one in which people expect most from others, and are least honest themselves.'
MARY CRAWFORD, *MANSFIELD PARK*, 1814

The public . . . is rather apt to be unreasonably discontented when a woman does marry again, than when she does not.
PERSUASION, 1818

'An engaged woman is always more agreeable than a disengaged. She is satisfied with herself. Her cares are over, and she feels that she may exert all her powers of pleasing without suspicion. All is safe with a lady engaged; no harm can be done.'
HENRY CRAWFORD, *MANSFIELD PARK*, 1814

That numerous class of females, whose society can raise no other emotion than surprise at there being any men in the world who could like them well enough to marry them.
NORTHANGER ABBEY, 1818

When any two young people take it into their heads to marry, they are pretty sure by perseverance to carry their point, be they ever so poor, or ever so imprudent, or ever so little likely to be necessary to each other's comfort.
PERSUASION, 1818

Matrimony, as the origin of change, was always disagreeable.
EMMA, 1816

Your news of Edward Bridges was *quite* news, for I have
had no letter from Wrotham. – I wish him happy with all
my heart, and hope his choice may turn out according to
his own expectations, and beyond those of his family –
and I dare say it will. Marriage is a great improver . . . As
to money, that will come, you may be sure, because they
cannot do without it.
LETTER TO CASSANDRA, 20 NOVEMBER 1808

'I pay very little regard to what any young
person says on the subject of marriage. If they
profess a disinclination for it, I only set it down
that they have not yet seen the right person.'
MRS GRANT, *MANSFIELD PARK*, 1814

On the subject of matrimony, I must notice a wedding in the Salisbury paper, which has amused me very much, Dr Phillot to Lady Frances St Lawrence. *She* wanted to have a husband I suppose, once in her life, and *he* a Lady Frances.
LETTER TO CASSANDRA, 24–5 OCTOBER 1808

'You could not have made me the offer of your hand in any possible way that would have tempted me to accept it.'
ELIZABETH BENNET, *PRIDE AND PREJUDICE*, 1813

'It is always incomprehensible to a man that a woman should ever refuse an offer of marriage. A man always imagines a woman to be ready for any body who asks her.'
EMMA, *EMMA*, 1816

'A lady's imagination is very rapid; it jumps from admiration to love, from love to matrimony in a moment.'
MR DARCY, *PRIDE AND PREJUDICE*, 1813

'Let him have all the perfections in the world, I think it ought not to be set down as certain that a man must be acceptable to every woman he may happen to like himself.'
FANNY, *MANSFIELD PARK*, 1814

'I had not known you a month before I felt that you were the last man in the world whom I could ever be prevailed on to marry.'
ELIZABETH BENNET, *PRIDE AND PREJUDICE*, 1813

Happily [Mr Woodhouse] was not farther from approving matrimony than from foreseeing it. – Though always objecting to every marriage that was arranged, he never suffered beforehand from the apprehension of any; it seemed as if he could not think so ill of any two persons' understanding as to suppose they meant to marry till it were proved against them.
EMMA, 1816

'People that marry can never part, but must go and keep house together. People that dance only stand opposite each other in a long room for half an hour.'
CATHERINE MORLAND, *NORTHANGER ABBEY*, 1818

Lady Sondes' match surprises, but does not offend me; had her first marriage been of affection, or had there been a grown-up single daughter, I should not have forgiven her; but I consider everybody as having a right to marry *once* in their lives for love, if they can, and provided she will now leave off having bad headaches and being pathetic, I can allow her, I can *wish* her, to be happy.
LETTER TO CASSANDRA, 27–8 DECEMBER 1808

Miss Bigg . . . writes me word that Miss Blachford *is* married. But I have never seen it in the paper. And one may as well be single, if the wedding is not to be in print.
LETTER TO ANNA LEFROY (AUSTEN),
LATE FEBRUARY/EARLY MARCH 1815

'And to marry for money I think the wickedest thing
in existence.'
CATHERINE MORLAND, *NORTHANGER ABBEY*, 1818

A good man must feel, how wretched, and how
unpardonable, how hopeless, and how wicked it was to marry
without affection.
MANSFIELD PARK, 1814

'Poverty is a great evil; but to a woman of
education and feeling it ought not, it cannot
be the greatest. I would rather be a teacher at a
school (and I can think of nothing worse) than
marry a man I did not like.'
EMMA, *THE WATSONS*, 1804

Anything is to be preferred or endured rather than marrying
without affection.
LETTER TO FANNY KNIGHT, 18 NOVEMBER 1814

Nothing can be compared to the misery of being bound
without love, bound to one, and preferring another.
LETTER TO FANNY KNIGHT, 30 NOVEMBER 1814

The Nature of Their Attachments:
Men and Women

The Nature of Their Attachments

'One cannot be always laughing at a man without now and then stumbling on something witty.'
ELIZABETH BENNET, *PRIDE AND PREJUDICE*, 1813

'I never heard a young lady spoken of for the first time without being informed that she was very accomplished.'
MR BINGLEY, *PRIDE AND PREJUDICE*, 1813

'If there is anything disagreeable going on men are always sure to get out of it.'
MARY MUSGROVE, *PERSUASION*, 1818

'I never in my life saw a man more intent on being agreeable than Mr Elton. It is downright labour to him where ladies are concerned. With men he can be rational and unaffected, but when he has ladies to please, every feature works.'
MR JOHN KNIGHTLEY, *EMMA*, 1816

'Man is more robust than woman, but he is not longer lived; which exactly explains my view of the nature of their attachments.'
ANNE ELLIOT, *PERSUASION*, 1818

'We certainly do not forget you as soon as you forget us.'
ANNE ELLIOT, *PERSUASION*, 1818

'I do not think I ever opened a book in my life which had not something to say upon woman's inconstancy. Songs and proverbs, all talk of woman's fickleness.'
MR HARVILLE, *PERSUASION*, 1818

'Men have had every advantage of us in telling their own story. Education has been theirs in so much higher a degree; the pen has been in their hands. I will not allow books to prove anything.'
ANNE ELLIOT, *PERSUASION*, 1818

'All the privilege I claim for my own sex (it is not a very enviable one; you need not covet it), is that of loving longest, when existence or when hope is gone.'
ANNE ELLIOT, *PERSUASION*, 1818

'So, Lizzy . . . your sister is crossed in love, I find. I congratulate her. Next to being married, a girl likes to be crossed in love a little now and then. It is something to think of, and gives her a sort of distinction among her companions.'
MR BENNET, *PRIDE AND PREJUDICE*, 1813

'But that expression of "violently in love" is so hackneyed, so doubtful, so indefinite, that it gives me very little idea. It is as often applied to feelings which arise from an half-hour's acquaintance, as to a real, strong attachment. Pray, how violent was Mr Bingley's love?'
MRS GARDINER, *PRIDE AND PREJUDICE*, 1813

'Is not general incivility the very essence of love?'
ELIZABETH BENNET, *PRIDE AND PREJUDICE*, 1813

'I think very highly of the understanding of all the women
in the world – especially of those – whoever they may be –
with whom I happen to be in company.'
HENRY TILNEY, *NORTHANGER ABBEY*, 1818

'That would be the greatest misfortune of all! – to find a man
agreeable whom one is determined to hate!'
ELIZABETH BENNET, *PRIDE AND PREJUDICE*, 1813

'You are too sensible a girl . . . to fall in love merely because
you are warned against it.'
MRS GARDINER, *PRIDE AND PREJUDICE*, 1813

[Anne Elliot] had been forced into prudence in her youth, she learned romance as she grew older: the natural sequel of an unnatural beginning.

PERSUASION, 1818

'If I loved you less, I might be able to talk about it more.'

MR KNIGHTLEY, *EMMA*, 1816

There are such beings in the world – perhaps one in a thousand – as the creature you and I should think perfection; where grace and spirit are united to worth, where the manners are equal to the heart and understanding; but such a person may not come in your way, or, if he does, he may not be the *eldest son* of a man of fortune, the near relation of your particular friend, and belonging to your own county.

LETTER TO FANNY KNIGHT, 18 NOVEMBER 1814

Love, they say, is like a rose;
I'm sure 'tis like the wind that blows,
For not a human creature knows
How it comes or where it goes.
It is the cause of many woes:
It swells the eyes and reds the nose,
And very often changes those
Who once were friends to bitter foes.
FROM ONE OF THE VERSES TO RHYME
WITH 'ROSE', 1807

Jane Austen In Love–And Not

I am almost afraid to tell you how my Irish friend and I behaved. Imagine to yourself everything most profligate and shocking in the way of dancing and sitting down together. I *can* expose myself however, only *once more*, because he leaves the country soon after next Friday, on which day we *are* to have a dance at Ashe after all. He is a very gentlemanlike, good-looking, pleasant young man, I assure you. But as to our having ever met, except at the three last balls, I cannot say much; for he is so excessively laughed at about me at Ashe, that he is ashamed of coming to Steventon, and ran away when we called on Mrs Lefroy a few days ago.

LETTER TO CASSANDRA, 9–10 JANUARY 1796

Our party to Ashe to-morrow night will consist of Edward Cooper, James (for a ball is nothing without *him*), Buller, who is now staying with us, and I. I look forward with great impatience to it, as I rather expect to receive an offer from my friend in the course of the evening. I shall refuse him, however, unless he promises to give away his white coat.

LETTER TO CASSANDRA, 14–15 JANUARY 1796

He has but one fault, which time will, I trust, entirely remove
– it is that his morning coat is a great deal too light.
LETTER TO CASSANDRA, 9–10 JANUARY 1796

Tell Mary that I make over Mr Heartley and all his estate to
her for her sole use and benefit in future, and not only him,
but all my other admirers into the bargain wherever she can
find them, even the kiss which C. Powlett wanted to give
me, as I mean to confine myself in future to Mr Tom Lefroy,
for whom I don't care sixpence. Assure her also, as a last and
indubitable proof of Warren's indifference to me, that he
actually drew that gentleman's picture for me, and delivered it
to me without a sigh.
LETTER TO CASSANDRA, 14–15 JANUARY 1796

At length the day is come on which I am to flirt my last with
Tom Lefroy, and when you receive this it will be over. My
tears flow at the melancholy idea.
LETTER TO CASSANDRA, 14–15 JANUARY 1796

'It would give me particular pleasure to have an opportunity of improving my acquaintance with that family – with a hope of creating to myself a nearer interest' – [*wrote Rev. Samuel Blackall to Mrs Lefroy. But he couldn't . . . Jane Austen was shown his letter and comments:*] This is rational enough; there is less love and more sense in it than sometimes appeared before, and I am very well satisfied. It will all go on exceedingly well, and decline away in a very reasonable manner.

There seems no likelihood of his [Blackall's] coming into Hampshire this Christmas, and it is therefore most probable that our indifference will soon be mutual, unless his regard, which appeared to spring from knowing nothing of me at first, is best supported by never seeing me.

LETTER TO CASSANDRA, 17 NOVEMBER 1798

And, years later:

I wonder whether you happened to see Mr Blackall's marriage in the papers last January? *We* did. He was married at Clifton to a Miss Lewis, whose father had been late of Antigua. I should very much like to know what sort of a woman she is. He was a piece of perfection, noisy perfection himself which I always recollect with regard . . . I would wish Miss Lewis to be of a silent turn and rather ignorant, but naturally intelligent and wishing to learn; – fond of cold veal pies, green tea in the afternoon, and a green window blind at night.

LETTER TO FRANK, ON HMS *ELEPHANT*, 3 JULY 1813

There was one gentleman, an officer of the Cheshire, a very good-looking young man, who, I was told, wanted very much to be introduced to me, but as he did not want it quite enough to take much trouble in effecting it, we never could bring it about.

LETTER TO CASSANDRA, 8 JANUARY 1799

Jane Austen had running jokes with her family about her marrying Rev. John Rawsthorne Papillon (a distant relative of the Knights and rector of Chawton) or the poet George Crabbe.

No, I have never seen [news of] the death of Mrs Crabbe. I have only just been making out from one of his prefaces that he probably was married ... Poor woman! I will comfort *him* as well as I can, but I do not undertake to be good to her children. She had better not leave any.

LETTER TO CASSANDRA, 21 DECEMBER 1813

She [Mrs Knight] may depend upon it that I *will* marry Mr Papillon, whatever may be his reluctance or my own.
LETTER TO CASSANDRA, 9 DECEMBER 1808

I am happy to tell you that Mr Papillon will soon make his offer, probably next Monday, as he returns on Saturday.
LETTER TO EIGHTEEN-YEAR-OLD EDWARD AUSTEN-LEIGH, 16–17 DECEMBER 1816

A Neighbourhood
of Voluntary Spies:
Friends and
Acquaintances

'For what do we live, but to make sport for our neighbours,
and laugh at them in our turn?'
MR BENNET, *PRIDE AND PREJUDICE*, 1813

'In a country like this, where social and literary intercourse
is on such a footing, where every man is surrounded by a
neighbourhood of voluntary spies.'
HENRY TILNEY, *NORTHANGER ABBEY*, 1818

Mr Richard Harvey is going to be married; but
as it is a great secret and only known to half the
neighbourhood, you must not mention it.
LETTER TO CASSANDRA, 5 SEPTEMBER 1796

Mr Children's two sons are both going to be married, John
and George. They are to have one wife between them, a Miss
Holwell, who belongs to the Black Hole at Calcutta.
LETTER TO CASSANDRA, 15–16 SEPTEMBER 1796

Mrs Hall of Sherbourn was brought to bed yesterday of a dead child, some weeks before she expected, owing to a fright. I suppose she happened unawares to look at her husband.
LETTER TO CASSANDRA, 27–8 OCTOBER 1798

Mrs Portman is not much admired in Dorsetshire; the good-natured world as usual extolled her beauty so highly that all the neighbourhood have had the pleasure of being disappointed.
LETTER TO CASSANDRA, 17–18 NOVEMBER 1798

Charles Powlett gave a dance on Thursday, to the great disturbance of all his neighbours, of course, who, you know, take a most lively interest in the state of his finances, and live in hopes of his being soon ruined.
LETTER TO CASSANDRA, 1–2 DECEMBER 1798

I do not want people to be very agreeable, as it saves me the trouble of liking them a great deal.

LETTER TO CASSANDRA, 24–6 DECEMBER 1798

I do not like the Miss Blackstones; indeed, I was always determined not to like them, so there is the less merit in it.

LETTER TO CASSANDRA, 8 JANUARY 1799

At the bottom of Kingsdown Hill we met a gentleman in a buggy, who, on a minute examination, turned out to be Dr Hall – and Dr Hall in such very deep mourning that either his mother, his wife, or himself must be dead.

LETTER TO CASSANDRA, 17 MAY 1799

I spent Friday evening with the Mapletons, and was obliged to submit to being pleased in spite of my inclination.

LETTER TO CASSANDRA, 2 JUNE 1799

Dr Gardiner was married yesterday to Mrs Percy and her three daughters.
LETTER TO CASSANDRA, 11 JUNE 1799

The Miss Maitlands are both prettyish . . . with brown skins, large dark eyes, and a good deal of nose. – The General has got the gout, and Mrs Maitland the jaundice. – Miss Debary, Susan and Sally . . . made their appearance, and I was as civil to them as their bad breath would allow me.
LETTER TO CASSANDRA, 20–1 NOVEMBER 1800

I cannot anyhow continue to find people agreeable; I respect Mrs Chamberlayne for doing her hair well, but cannot feel a more tender sentiment. Miss Langley is like any other short girl, with a broad nose and wide mouth, fashionable dress and exposed bosom. Adm. Stanhope is a gentleman-like man, but then his legs are too short and his tail too long.
LETTER TO CASSANDRA, 12–13 MAY 1801

Unluckily however, I see nothing to be glad of, unless I make
it a matter of joy that Mrs Wylmot has another son, and that
Lord Lucan has taken a mistress, both of which events are of
course joyful to the actors [the participants].
LETTER TO CASSANDRA, 8–9 FEBRUARY 1807

We are to have a tiny party here tonight; I
hate tiny parties – they force one into constant
exertion. – Miss Edwards and her father, Mrs
Busby and her nephew Mr Maitland, and Mrs
Lillingstone are to be the whole; – and I am
prevented from setting my black cap at Mr
Maitland by his having a wife and ten children. –
My aunt has a very bad cough: do not forget to
have heard about *that* when you come . . .
LETTER TO CASSANDRA, 21–2 MAY 1808

We drink tea tonight with Mrs Busby – I
scandalized her nephew cruelly; he has but three
children instead of ten.
'PS' TO THE ABOVE

I shall not tell you anything more of William Digweed's china, as your silence on the subject makes you unworthy of it.

LETTER TO CASSANDRA, 27–8 DECEMBER 1808

Mr Digweed has used us basely. Handsome is as handsome does; he is therefore a very ill-looking man.

LETTER TO CASSANDRA, 24 JANUARY 1813

How horrible it is to have so many people killed! And what a blessing that one cares for none of them!

LETTER TO CASSANDRA ON THE PENINSULAR WAR,
31 MAY 1811

If Mrs Freeman is anywhere above ground give my best compliments to her.

LETTER TO CASSANDRA, 9 FEBRUARY 1813

He seems a very harmless sort of young man, nothing to like or dislike in him – goes out shooting or hunting with the two others all the morning, and plays at whist and makes queer faces in the evening.

LETTER TO CASSANDRA, 23–4 SEPTEMBER 1813

Only think of Mrs Holder's being dead! Poor woman, she has done the only thing in the world she could possibly do to make one cease to abuse her.

LETTER TO CASSANDRA, 14–15 OCTOBER 1813

We have got rid of Mr R. Mascall, however. I did not like *him* either. He talks too much, and is conceited, besides having a vulgarly shaped mouth.

LETTER TO CASSANDRA, 14–15 OCTOBER 1813

The Webbs are really gone! When I saw the waggons at the door, and thought of all the trouble they must have in moving, I began to reproach myself for not having liked them better – but since the waggons have disappeared my conscience has been closed again, and I am excessively glad they are gone.

LETTER TO ANNA AUSTEN, 28 SEPTEMBER 1814

Poor woman! how can she honestly be breeding again?

LETTER TO CASSANDRA ON ONE MRS TILSON,
1–2 OCTOBER 1808

I would recommend to her and Mr D. the simple regimen of separate rooms.

LETTER TO FANNY KNIGHT ON THEIR FRIEND MRS DEEDES
GIVING BIRTH, 20–1 FEBRUARY 1817

Vanity Working on a Weak Head: Affectation and Arrogance

Their vanity was in such good order that they seemed to be quite free from it.
MANSFIELD PARK, 1814

Vanity was the beginning and the end of Sir Walter Elliot's character; vanity of person and of situation.
PERSUASION, 1818

'Vanity working on a weak head, produces every sort of mischief.'
MR KNIGHTLEY, *EMMA*, 1816

It was a struggle between propriety and vanity; but vanity got the better.
PERSUASION, 1818

'It is very often nothing but our own vanity that deceives us.
Women fancy admiration means more than it does.'
JANE BENNET, *PRIDE AND PREJUDICE*, 1813

'A man . . . must have a very good opinion of himself when
he asks people to leave their own fireside, and encounter
such a day as this, for the sake of coming to see him. He must
think himself a most agreeable fellow; I could not do such a
thing. It is the greatest absurdity.'
MR JOHN KNIGHTLEY, *EMMA*, 1816

Sir Edward's great object in life was to be seductive.
– With such personal advantages as he knew
himself to possess, and such talents as he did also
give himself credit for, he regarded it as his duty.
– He felt that he was formed to be a dangerous
man – quite in the line of the Lovelaces. – The very
name of 'Sir Edward', he thought, carried some
degree of fascination with it.
SANDITON, 1817

She had not been brought up . . . to know to how many
idle assertions and impudent falsehoods the excess of
vanity will lead.
NORTHANGER ABBEY, 1818

Mrs Breton called here on Saturday. I never saw her before.
She is a large, ungenteel woman, with self-satisfied and
would-be elegant manners.
LETTER TO CASSANDRA, 11–12 OCTOBER 1813

Dr Breton['s] . . . wife amuses me very much with her
affected refinement and elegance.
LETTER TO CASSANDRA, 6–7 NOVEMBER 1813

She had prejudices on the side of ancestry; she had a value for
rank and consequence, which blinded her a little to the faults
of those who possessed them.
PERSUASION, 1818, OF LADY RUSSELL

'Lady Catherine herself says that, in point of true beauty, Miss de Bourgh is far superior to the handsomest of her sex; because there is that in her features which marks the young woman of distinguished birth.'
MR COLLINS, *PRIDE AND PREJUDICE*, 1813

'Do not make yourself uneasy, my dear cousin, about your apparel. Lady Catherine is far from requiring that elegance of dress in us, which becomes herself and daughter. I would advise you merely to put on whatever of your clothes is superior to the rest, there is no occasion for anything more. Lady Catherine will not think the worse of you for being simply dressed. She likes to have the distinction of rank preserved.'
MR COLLINS, *PRIDE AND PREJUDICE*, 1813

[Lady Catherine's] air was not conciliating, nor was her manner of receiving them such as to make her visitors forget their inferior rank.
PRIDE AND PREJUDICE, 1813

There was little to be done but to hear Lady Catherine talk, which she did without any intermission till coffee came in, delivering her opinion on every subject in so decisive a manner, as proved that she was not used to have her judgment controverted.
PRIDE AND PREJUDICE, 1813

Elizabeth found that nothing was beneath this great lady's attention, which could furnish her with an occasion of dictating to others.
PRIDE AND PREJUDICE, 1813

Lady Middleton could no longer endure such a conversation, and therefore exerted herself to ask Mr Palmer if there was any news in the paper. 'No, none at all,' he replied, and read on.
SENSE AND SENSIBILITY, 1811

A Mr (save, perhaps, some half dozen in the nation,)
always needs a note of explanation.
PERSUASION, 1818

'My love, you contradict every body,' said his wife with her
usual laugh. 'Do you know that you are quite rude?'
'I did not know I contradicted any body in calling
your mother ill-bred.'
SENSE AND SENSIBILITY, 1811

Still Mrs Norris was at intervals urging something different;
and in the most interesting moment of his passage to
England, when the alarm of a French privateer was at the
height, she burst through his recital with the proposal of soup.
'Sure, my dear Sir Thomas, a basin of soup would be a much
better thing for you than tea. Do have a basin of soup.'
MANSFIELD PARK, 1814

'Nothing is more deceitful than the appearance of humility. It is often only carelessness of opinion, and sometimes an indirect boast.'
MR DARCY, *PRIDE AND PREJUDICE*, 1813

'It is very difficult for the prosperous to be humble.'
FRANK CHURCHILL, *EMMA*, 1816

'Selfishness must always be forgiven, you know, because there is no hope of a cure.'
MARY CRAWFORD, *MANSFIELD PARK*, 1814

'People who suffer as I do from nervous complaints can have no great inclination for talking. Nobody can tell what I suffer! But it is always so. Those who do not complain are never pitied.'
MRS BENNET, *PRIDE AND PREJUDICE*, 1813

'I dare say I shall catch it; and my sore-throats, you know, are always worse than anybody's.'
MARY MUSGRAVE, *PERSUASION*, 1818

'You take delight in vexing me. You have no compassion on my poor nerves.'
'You mistake me, my dear. I have a high respect for your nerves. They are my old friends. I have heard you mention them with consideration these twenty years at least.'
MR AND MRS BENNET, *PRIDE AND PREJUDICE*, 1813

The Dissipations
of London,
the Luxuries of Bath

'Alas! (exclaimed I) how am I to avoid those evils I shall never be exposed to? What probability is there of my ever tasting the dissipations of London, the luxuries of Bath, or the stinking fish of Southampton? I who am doomed to waste my Days of Youth and Beauty in an humble cottage in the Vale of Uske.'

LAURA, *LOVE AND FREINDSHIP*, 1790

'One has not great hopes from Birmingham. I always say there is something direful in the sound.'

MRS ELTON, *EMMA*, 1816

'Oh! Who can ever be tired of Bath?'
. . . Catherine was so hopeful a scholar that when they gained the top of Beechen Cliff, she voluntarily rejected the whole city of Bath as unworthy to make part of a landscape.

NORTHANGER ABBEY, 1818

The first view of Bath in fine weather does not answer my expectations; I think I see more distinctly through rain. The sun was got behind everything, and the appearance of the place from the top of Kingsdown was all vapour, shadow, smoke, and confusion.

LETTER TO CASSANDRA, 5–6 MAY 1801

'Every five years, one hears of some new place or other starting up by the sea and growing the fashion. How they can half of them be filled is the wonder! Where people can be found with money and time to go to them!'

MR HEYWOOD, *SANDITON*, 1817

'We do not look in great cities for our best morality.'

EDMUND BERTRAM, *MANSFIELD PARK*, 1814

The language of London is flat.

LETTER TO MARTHA LLOYD, 2 SEPTEMBER 1814

'The truth is, that in London it is always a sickly season.
Nobody is healthy in London, nobody can be.'
MR WOODHOUSE, *EMMA*, 1816

Miss Middleton seems very happy, but has not beauty enough
to figure in London.
LETTER TO CASSANDRA, 25 APRIL 1811

Here I am once more in this scene of dissipation and vice,
and I begin already to find my morals corrupted.
LETTER TO CASSANDRA ON ARRIVING IN LONDON,
23 AUGUST 1796

'Wherever you are you should always be contented, but
especially at home, because there you must spend the most of
your time. I did not quite like, at breakfast, to hear you talk so
much about the French bread at Northanger.'
MRS MORLAND, *NORTHANGER ABBEY*, 1818

A Fine Family

'Nobody, who has not been in the interior of a family, can say what the difficulties of any individual of that family may be.'
EMMA, *EMMA*, 1816

Miss Frances married, in the common phrase, to disoblige her family, and by fixing on a lieutenant of marines, without education, fortune, or connexions, did it very thoroughly.
MANSFIELD PARK, 1814

'Family squabbling is the greatest evil of all, and we had better do anything than be altogether by the ears.'
EDMUND BERTRAM, *MANSFIELD PARK*, 1814

Children of the same family, the same blood, with the same first associations and habits, have some means of enjoyment in their power, which no subsequent connexions can supply.
MANSFIELD PARK, 1814

A family of ten children will be always called a fine family,
where there are heads and arms and legs enough for
the number.
NORTHANGER ABBEY, 1818

I shall think with tenderness and delight on his beautiful and
smiling countenance and interesting manner, until a few years
have turned him into an ungovernable, ungracious fellow.
LETTER TO CASSANDRA, ON ONE OF THEIR NEPHEWS,
27–8 OCTOBER 1798

I expected to have heard from you this morning,
but no letter is come. I shall not take the trouble
of announcing to you any more of Mary's
children, if, instead of thanking me for the
intelligence, you always sit down and write to
James. I am sure nobody can desire your letters
so much as I do, and I don't think anybody
deserves them so well.
LETTER TO CASSANDRA, 25 NOVEMBER 1798

A Fine Family

A lady, without a family, was the very best preserver of
furniture in the world.
PERSUASION, 1818

My mother looks forward with as much certainty as you can
do to our keeping two maids . . . We plan having a steady
cook and a young, giddy housemaid, with a sedate, middle-
aged man, who is to undertake the double office of husband
to the former and sweetheart to the latter. No children, of
course, to be allowed on either side.
LETTER TO CASSANDRA, 3–5 JANUARY 1801

You are very kind in planning presents for me to make, and
my mother has shown me exactly the same attention; but as
I do not choose to have generosity dictated to me, I shall not
resolve on giving my cabinet to Anna till the first thought of
it has been my own.
LETTER TO CASSANDRA, 8–9 JANUARY 1801

You will have a great deal of unreserved discourse with Mrs K., I dare say, upon this subject, as well as upon many other of our family matters. Abuse everybody but me.

Letter to Cassandra, 7–8 January 1807

Cousin Fanny Austen's match is quite news, and I am sorry she has behaved so ill. There is some comfort to us in her misconduct, that we have not a congratulatory letter to write.

Letter to Cassandra, 30 June – 1 July 1808

I tell you everything, and it is unknown the mysteries you conceal from me; and, to add to the rest, you persevere in giving a final *e* to invalid, thereby putting it out of one's power to suppose Mrs E. Leigh, even for a moment, a veteran soldier.

Letter to Cassandra, 24 January 1809

The Portsmouth paper gave a melancholy history of a poor mad woman, escaped from confinement, who said her husband and daughter, of the name of Payne, lived at Ashford, in Kent. Do you own them?

LETTER TO CASSANDRA, 24 JANUARY 1809

I give you joy of our new nephew, and hope if he ever comes to be hanged it will not be till we are too old to care about it.

LETTER TO CASSANDRA, 25 APRIL 1811

I take it for granted that Mary has told you of Anna's engagement to Ben Lefroy. It came upon us without much preparation; – at the same time, there was *that* about her which kept us in a constant preparation for something.

LETTER TO FRANK, 25 SEPTEMBER 1813

My dearest Aunt Cass,
I have just asked Aunt Jane to let me write a little in her
letter, but she does not like it, so I won't – good-bye.
Fanny Knight in JA's Letter to Cassandra,
11–12 October 1813

I am to meet Mrs Harrison, and we are to talk about Ben
and Anna. 'My dear Mrs Harrison,' I shall say, 'I am afraid the
young man has some of your family madness, and though
there often appears to be something of madness in Anna too,
I think she inherits more of it from her mother's family than
from ours.' That is what I shall say, and I think she will find
it difficult to answer me.
Letter to Cassandra, 3 November 1813

Mrs F. A. seldom either looks or appears quite well. Little
Embryo is troublesome, I suppose.
Letter to Cassandra, 8–9 September 1814
(Mrs F. A. was Frank's wife, Mary.)

I rather imagine indeed that nieces are seldom chosen but
out of compliment to some aunt or another.
LETTER TO ANNA LEFROY (AUSTEN), 30 NOVEMBER 1814

Now that you are become an aunt, you are a person of some
consequence and must excite great interest whatever you do.
I have always maintained the importance of aunts as much as
possible, and I am sure of your doing the same now.
LETTER TO TEN-YEAR-OLD CAROLINE AUSTEN,
30 OCTOBER 1815

The pianoforte often talks of you; – in various keys, tunes and
expressions I allow – but be it lesson or country dance, sonata
or waltz, *you* are really its constant theme.
LETTER TO TWELVE-YEAR-OLD CAROLINE AUSTEN,
23 JANUARY 1817

Ben and Anna walked here . . . and she looked so pretty, it was quite a pleasure to see her, so young and so blooming, and so innocent, as if she had never had a wicked thought in her life, which yet one has some reason to suppose she must have had, if we believe the doctrine of original sin or if we remember the events of her girlish days.

LETTER TO FANNY KNIGHT, 20–1 FEBRUARY 1817

Anna has not a chance of escape; her husband called here the other day, and said she was *pretty* well but not equal to so long a walk; she *must come in* her *donkey carriage*. Poor Animal, she will be worn out before she is thirty. – I am very sorry for her. Mrs Clement too is in that way again. I am quite tired of so many children. – Mrs Benn has a 13th.

LETTER TO FANNY KNIGHT, 23–5 MARCH 1817

One Half Cannot
Understand the
Other: Observations
General and
Particular

She had nothing against her but her husband and
her conscience.
LADY SUSAN, ?1793–5

'People who suffer as I do from nervous complaints can
have no great inclination for talking . . .' She [Mrs Bennet]
talked on.
PRIDE AND PREJUDICE, 1813

I looked at Sir Thomas Champneys and thought of poor
Rosalie; I looked at his daughter, and thought her a queer
animal with a white neck.
LETTER TO CASSANDRA, 20–1 NOVEMBER 1800

Mr Robert Mascall . . . eats a great deal of butter.
LETTER TO CASSANDRA, 11–12 OCTOBER 1813

[Mr Lushington, MP, MF] is quite an MP – very smiling,
with an exceeding good address, and readiness of language . . .
I dare say he is ambitious and insincere.
LETTER TO CASSANDRA, 14–15 OCTOBER 1813

[Mrs Bennet] was a woman of mean understanding, little
information, and uncertain temper.
PRIDE AND PREJUDICE, 1813

A person and face, of strong, natural, sterling insignificance.
SENSE AND SENSIBILITY, 1811

Mrs Bennet was restored to her usual querulous serenity.
PRIDE AND PREJUDICE, 1813

[Mrs Ferrars] was not a woman of many words;
for, unlike people in general, she proportioned
them to the number of her ideas.
SENSE AND SENSIBILITY, 1811

He knew her illnesses; they never occurred but for her
own convenience.
EMMA, 1816

[Miss Bates] enjoyed a most uncommon degree of popularity
for a woman neither young, handsome, rich, nor married.
EMMA, 1816

Mrs Norris was one of those well-meaning people who are
always doing mistaken and very disagreeable things.
MANSFIELD PARK, 1814

'Mr Wickham is blessed with such happy manners as may ensure his making friends: whether he may be equally capable of retaining them is less certain.'
ELIZABETH BENNET, *PRIDE AND PREJUDICE*, 1813

I will not say that your mulberry-trees are dead, but I am afraid they are not alive.
LETTER TO CASSANDRA, 31 MAY 1811

'One half of the world cannot understand the pleasures of the other.'
EMMA, *EMMA*, 1816

'Why not seize the pleasure at once? How often is happiness destroyed by preparation, foolish preparation!'
FRANK CHURCHILL, *EMMA*, 1816

'The pleasantness of an employment does not always
evince its propriety.'
ELINOR DASHWOOD, *SENSE AND SENSIBILITY*, 1811

'The more I see of the world, the more am I dissatisfied with
it; and every day confirms my belief of the inconsistency of
all human characters, and of the little dependence that can be
placed on the appearance of either merit or sense.'
ELIZABETH BENNET, *PRIDE AND PREJUDICE*, 1813

Seldom, very seldom, does complete truth belong to any
human disclosure; seldom can it happen that something is not
a little disguised, or a little mistaken; but where, as in this case,
though the conduct is mistaken, the feelings are not, it
may not be very material.
EMMA, 1816

'It is particularly incumbent on those who never change their opinion to be secure of judging properly at first.'
ELIZABETH BENNET, *PRIDE AND PREJUDICE*, 1813

To look almost pretty is an acquisition of higher delight to a girl who has been looking plain the first fifteen years of her life than a beauty from her cradle can ever receive.
NORTHANGER ABBEY, 1818

'Think only of the past as its remembrance gives you pleasure.'
ELIZABETH BENNET, *PRIDE AND PREJUDICE*, 1813

'I do not know whether it ought to be so, but certainly silly things do cease to be silly if they are done by sensible people in an impudent way. Wickedness is always wickedness, but folly is not always folly. – It depends upon the character of those who handle it.'
EMMA, *EMMA*, 1816

Where people wish to attach, they should always
be ignorant. To come with a well-informed mind
is to come with an inability of administering
to the vanity of others, which a sensible person
would always wish to avoid. A woman especially,
if she have the misfortune of knowing anything,
should conceal it as well as she can.
NORTHANGER ABBEY, 1818

'But your mind is warped by an innate principle of general
integrity, and therefore not accessible to the cool reasonings
of family partiality, or a desire of revenge.'
HENRY TILNEY, *NORTHANGER ABBEY*, 1818

The real evils, indeed, of Emma's situation were the power
of having rather too much her own way, and a disposition to
think a little too well of herself.
EMMA, 1816

How quick come the reasons for approving what we like!
PERSUASION, 1818

'It is the worst evil of too yielding and indecisive a character, that no influence over it can be depended on. You are never sure of a good impression being durable; everybody may sway it. Let those who would be happy be firm.'
CAPTAIN WENTWORTH, *PERSUASION*, 1818

'It is a most repulsive quality, indeed. Oftentimes very convenient, no doubt, but never pleasing. There is safety in reserve, but no attraction. One cannot love a reserved person.'
FRANK CHURCHILL, *EMMA*, 1816

'Surprises are foolish things. The pleasure is not enhanced, and the inconvenience is often considerable.'
MR KNIGHTLEY, *EMMA*, 1816

'Where so many hours have been spent in convincing
myself that I am right, is there not some reason to fear
I may be wrong?'
COLONEL BRANDON, *SENSE AND SENSIBILITY*, 1811

'The memory is sometimes so retentive, so serviceable, so
obedient; at others, so bewildered and so weak; and at others
again, so tyrannic, so beyond control! We are, to be sure, a
miracle every way; but our powers of recollecting and of
forgetting do seem peculiarly past finding out.'
FANNY, *MANSFIELD PARK,* 1814

'Where an opinion is general, it is usually correct.'
MARY CRAWFORD, *MANSFIELD PARK*, 1814

Emma denied none of it aloud,
and agreed to none of it in private.
EMMA, 1816

An occasional memento of past folly, however painful, might
not be without use.
NORTHANGER ABBEY, 1818

There are people, who the more you do for them, the less
they will do for themselves.
EMMA, 1816

'To be always firm must be to be often obstinate.'
HENRY TILNEY, *NORTHANGER ABBEY*, 1818

She felt she was in the greatest danger of being exquisitely
happy, while so many were miserable.
MANSFIELD PARK, 1814

'It will be a bitter pill to her; that is, like other bitter pills, it will have two moments' ill-flavour, and then be swallowed and forgotten.'
HENRY CRAWFORD, *MANSFIELD PARK*, 1814

'Our pleasures in this world are always to be paid for.'
HENRY TILNEY, *NORTHANGER ABBEY*, 1818

. . . in that inconvenient tone of voice which was perfectly audible while it pretended to be a whisper.
PERSUASION, 1818

'The kind of man . . . whom every body speaks well of, and nobody cares about; whom all are delighted to see, and nobody remembers to talk to.'
WILLOUGHBY, *SENSE AND SENSIBILITY*, 1811

With such a reward [*sugar plums*] for her tears, the child was too wise to cease crying.
SENSE AND SENSIBILITY, 1811

The old, well-established grievance of duty against will, parent against child.
PERSUASION, 1818

From politics, it was an easy step to silence.
NORTHANGER ABBEY, 1818

It is not time or opportunity that is to determine intimacy;
– It is disposition alone. Seven years would be insufficient to make some people acquainted with each other, and seven days are more than enough for others.
SENSE AND SENSIBILITY, 1811

One Half Cannot Understand the Other

After long thought and much perplexity, to be very brief was
all that she could determine on with any confidence of safety.
NORTHANGER ABBEY, 1818

He had just compunction enough for having done nothing
for his sisters himself, to be exceedingly anxious that
everybody else should do a great deal.
SENSE AND SENSIBILITY, 1811

Mr Wickham, who had charmed everybody with his pleasant
conversation, graceful manners and good looks,
was discovered to be a dishonest rascal interested primarily
in money . . . Everybody declared that he was the wickedest
young man in the world; and everybody began to find out,
that they had always distrusted the appearance of
his goodness.
PRIDE AND PREJUDICE, 1813

'A man who has nothing to do with his own time has no conscience in his intrusion on that of others.'
MARIANNE DASHWOOD, *SENSE AND SENSIBILITY*, 1811

Like half the rest of the world, if more than half there be that are clever and good, Marianne, with excellent abilities and an excellent disposition, was neither reasonable nor candid. She expected from other people the same opinions and feelings as her own, and she judged of their motives by the immediate effect of their actions on herself.
SENSE AND SENSIBILITY, 1811

'You ought certainly to forgive them as a Christian, but never to admit them in your sight, or allow their names to be mentioned in your hearing.'
MR COLLINS, *PRIDE AND PREJUDICE*, 1813

'I am particularly unlucky in meeting with a person so well able to expose my real character, in a part of the world, where I had hoped to pass myself off with some degree of credit.'
ELIZABETH BENNET, *PRIDE AND PREJUDICE*, 1813

He is a rogue of course, but a civil one.
LETTER TO CASSANDRA ON JOHN MURRAY, JA'S LAST PUBLISHER, 17–18 OCTOBER 1815

I Am a Very Good Housekeeper

My mother desires me to tell you that I am a very good housekeeper, which I have no reluctance in doing, because I really think it my peculiar excellence, and for this reason — I always take care to provide such things as please my own appetite, which I consider as the chief merit in housekeeping.
LETTER TO CASSANDRA, 17–18 NOVEMBER 1798

... such weather as gives one little temptation to be out. It is really too bad, and has been too bad for a long time, much worse than any one *can* bear, and I begin to think it will never be fine again. This is a *finesse* of mine, for I have often observed that if one writes about the weather, it is generally completely changed before the letter is read.
LETTER TO EDWARD AUSTEN-LEIGH, 9 JULY 1816

Your letter is come; it came indeed twelve lines ago, but I could not stop to acknowledge it before, and I am glad it did not arrive till I had completed my first sentence, because the sentence had been made since yesterday, and I think forms a very good beginning.
LETTER TO CASSANDRA, 1 NOVEMBER 1800

You express so little anxiety about my being murdered under Ash Park Copse by Mrs Hulbert's servant, that I have a great mind not to tell you whether I was or not.
LETTER TO CASSANDRA, 8–9 JANUARY 1799

Expect a most agreeable letter, for not being overburdened with subject (having nothing at all to say), I shall have no check to my genius from beginning to end.
LETTER TO CASSANDRA, 21 JANUARY 1801

I am forced to be abusive for want of subject, having really nothing to say.
LETTER TO CASSANDRA, 20-2 FEBRUARY 1807

You know how interesting the purchase of a sponge-cake is to me.
LETTER TO CASSANDRA, 15 JUNE 1808

Our ball was rather more amusing than I expected
. . . The melancholy part was, to see so many dozen
young women standing by without partners, and
each of them with two ugly naked shoulders! It was
the same room in which we danced fifteen years
ago! I thought it all over, and in spite of the shame
of being so much older, felt with thankfulness that I
was quite as happy now as then.

LETTER TO CASSANDRA, 9 DECEMBER 1808

[I] am very well satisfied with his notice of me – 'A pleasing
looking young woman' – that must do; one cannot pretend to
anything better now; thankful to have it continued a
few years longer!

LETTER TO CASSANDRA, 30 APRIL 1811

By the bye, as I must leave off being young, I find many
douceurs in being a sort of chaperon for I am put on the sofa
near the fire and can drink as much wine as I like.

LETTER TO CASSANDRA, 6 NOVEMBER 1813

You deserve a longer letter than this; but it is my unhappy fate seldom to treat people so well as they deserve.
LETTER TO CASSANDRA, 24–6 DECEMBER 1798

I am sorry my mother has been suffering, and am afraid this exquisite weather is too good to agree with her. I enjoy it all over me, from top to toe, from right to left, longitudinally, perpendicularly, diagonally; and I cannot but selfishly hope we are to have it last till Christmas – nice, unwholesome, unseasonable, relaxing, close, muggy weather.
LETTER TO CASSANDRA, 2 DECEMBER 1815

I am considerably better now and am recovering my looks a little, which have been bad enough – black and white, and every wrong colour. I must not depend upon being ever very blooming again. Sickness is a dangerous indulgence at my time of life.
LETTER TO FANNY KNIGHT, 23–5 MARCH 1817

Works by Jane Austen

Austen's main novels, as well as her works of short and unfinished fiction are listed here. Only a small selection of her early works and none of her reviews or letters are listed.

NOVELS
Sense and Sensibility, 1811
Pride and Prejudice, 1813
Mansfield Park, 1814
Emma, 1815
Northanger Abbey, 1818 (posthumous)
Persuasion, 1818 (posthumous)

SHORT FICTION
Lady Susan, 1794, 1805

UNFINISHED FICTION
The Watsons, 1804
Sanditon, 1817

OTHER WORKS
Sir Charles Grandison, 1793, 1800
Plan of a Novel, 1815

JUVENILIA

Frederic and Elfrida

Jack and Alice

Edgar and Emma

Henry and Eliza: A Novel

The Adventures of Mr Harley

Sir William Montague

Memoirs of Mr Clifford

Amelia Webster

The Visit: A Comedy in Two Acts

The Mystery: An Unfinished Play

Ode to Pity

Love and Freindship

Lesley Castle: An Unfinished Novel in Letters

The History of England

A Letter from a Young Lady

The Beautifull Cassandra

The Three Sisters

Evelyn

Catharine